example	exemple
Beispiel	
ejemplo	пример

This is an example of a bird.

fresh	frais
frisch	
fresco	свежий

All the fruit is fresh.

ball	balle
Ball	
pelota	мяч

He is bouncing the ball.

doll	poupée

Puppe

muñeca	кукла

She is hugging her doll.

home	maison

Zuhause

casa	дом

He drew a picture of his home.

way	façon

Weg

camino	путь

They find a way back home.

wind · vent

Wind

viento · ветер

The wind blows the leaves.

girl · fille

Mädchen

niña · девушка *девочка*

The girl is pretty.

farm · ferme

Bauernhof

granja · ферма

The farm has lots of animals.

seed   la graine

Samen

semilla   семя

We will plant the seeds.

---

shoe   chaussure

Schuh

zapato   башмак
                         обувь

I have new shoes.

---

party   fête

Party

fiesta   партия
                         праздник

I love to go to parties.

tree	arbre
Baum	
árbol	дерево

She is sitting under a tree.

---

window	fenêtre
Fenster	
ventana	окно

The window is open.

---

hill	colline
Hügel	
colina	холм

The house is on the hill.

kitty minou

Kitty

gatito ~~Китти~~
Кошечка

I like my kitty.

---

four quatre

vier

cuatro четыре

There were four of them.

---

sun soleil

Sonne

dom солнце

The sun is very bright.

place	endroit
Ort	
sitio	мест место
This is my favorite place.	

page	page
Seite	
página	страница
Please turn the page.	

brother	frère
Bruder	
hermano	брат
They are brothers.	

song   chanson

Lied

canciones   песня
    песни

She is singing a song.

thing   chose

Ding
Sache

cosa   предмет

I am thinking of many things.

cotton   coton

Baumwolle

algodón   хлопок

A q-tip is made of cotton.

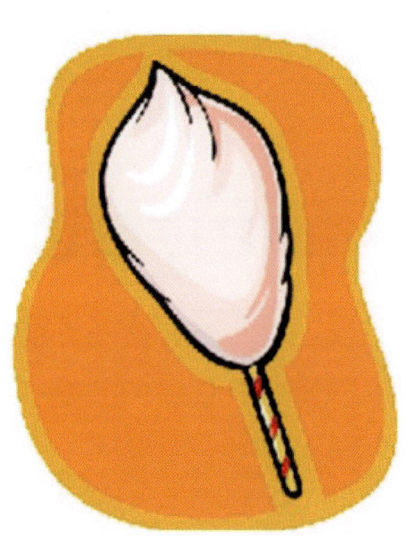

company	compagnie

Unternehmen

empresa — Компания

What company do you work for?

cake	gâteau

Kuchen

pastel — торт

The cake is white and pink.

father	père

Vater

papá — папа

He is a nice father.

bread   pain

Brot

un pan   хлеб

She is baking some bread.

milk   lait

Milch

leche   молоко

The baby is drinking milk.

snow   neige

Schnee

nieve   снег

I have fun in the snow.

food	aliments	
Essen		
comida	питание	

They made a lot of food.

---

dog	chien	
Hund		
perro	собака	

The dog wants to eat sweets.

---

conditions	conditions	
Bedingungen		
condiciones	условия	

What are the weather conditions.

France	france

Frankreich

francia   Франция

Have you ever been to France?

---

goodbye   au revoir

Auf
Wiedersehen

adiós   Прощай

The bear is saying goodbye.

---

head   tête

Kopf

cabeza   глава
голова

She has a hat on her head.

cat   chat

Katze

gato   кошка

That cat is adorable.

---

street   rue

Straße

calle   улица

They walk across the street.

---

feet   pieds

Füße

pies   ноги Beine
             стопы

His feet are swollen.

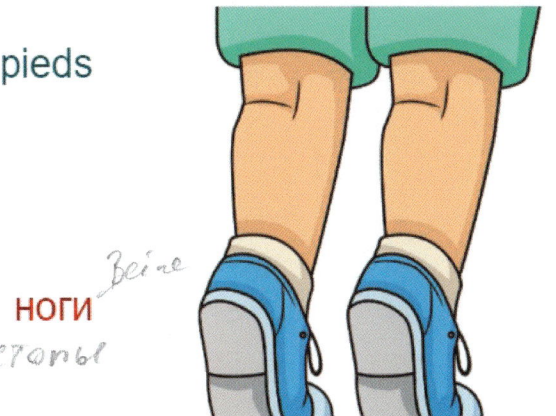

chair		chaises
Stühle		
sillas		стулья

He is sitting on the chair.

church		église
Kirche		
iglesia		церковь

Did you go to church?

hoe		houe
Hacke		
azada		мотыга

Use a hoe in the garden.

name	nom
Name	
nombre	имя

My name is Joe.

table	table
Tabelle	
mesa	Таблица

There is a toy on the table.

Tisch
стол

fish	poisson
Fisch	
pez	рыба

There are two fish.

boy		garçon
	Junge	
chico		мальчик

The boy is eating dinner.

nose		nez
	Nase	
nariz		нос

My nose is running.

box		boîte
	Box	
caja		коробка

The box is full of clothes.

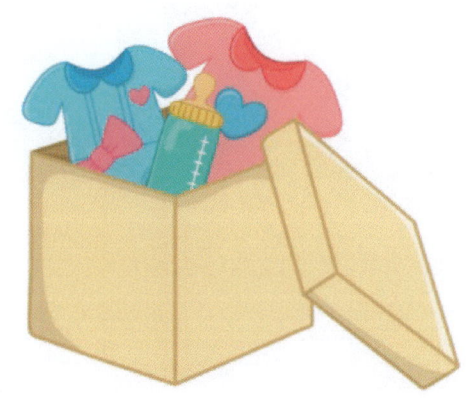

rose   rose

Rose

rosa   Роза

Thank you for the rose.

---

coat   manteau

Mantel

saco   Пальто

She is wearing her coat.

---

car   voiture

Auto

coche   машина

My car is fast

picture	image

Bild

imagen	рисунок

картина

He is taking some pictures.

grass	herbe

Gras

césped	трава

The goat is eating the grass.

bell	cloche

Glocke

campana	колокол

I hear the bell ringing!

mother	mère
Mutter	
madre	мама

My mother loves me.

bear	ours
Bär	
oso	нести

медведь

The bear likes to eat honey.

chicken	poulet
Hähnchen	
pollo	курица

The chicken is laying eggs.

rain	pluie
Regen	
lluvia	дождь

We love the rain!

horse	cheval
Pferd	
caballo	лошадь

The horse is galloping.

water	l'eau
Wasser	
agua	вода

He is drinking water.

idea idée

Idee

idea идея

I have an idea!

---

eye œil

Auge

ojo глаз

He is closing his eyes.

---

office bureau

Büro

oficina офис

Do you need any office supplies?

morning matin

Morgen

mañana утро

I wake up in the morning.

---

game jeu

Spiel

juegos игры

What game is it?

---

duck canard

Ente

pato утка

The duck is swimming.

family	famille
Familie	
familia	семья
How big is your family?	

Greek	grec
griechisch	
griego	греческий
Have you ever had Greek food?	

money	argent
Geld	
dinero	Деньги
I save money in my piggy bank.	

cow	vache	

Kuh

vaca · корова

The cow is standing up.

---

robin · robin

Robin

robin · Робин

The robin is helping Santa.

---

toy · jouet

Spielzeug

juguete · игрушка

He has a whole box of toys.

nest   nid

Nest

nido   гнездо

The bird has a nest.

---

score   but

Ergebnis

puntuación   Гол

What was the final score?

---

ground   sol

Boden

suelo   земля

It plays a trick on the ground.

top	haut
oben	
tapas	Вверх

We like to play with tops.

---

oxygen	oxygène
Sauerstoff	
oxígeno	кислород

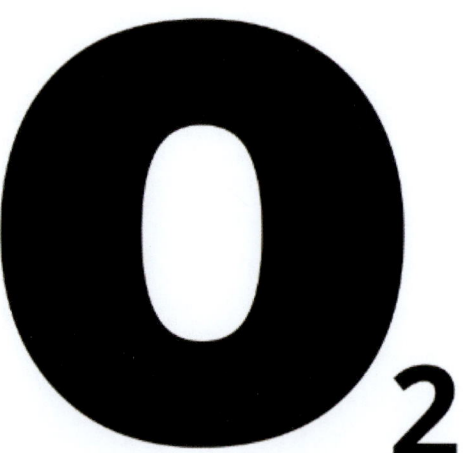

What is the symbol for oxygen?

---

gun	pistolet
Gewehr	
pistola	оружие

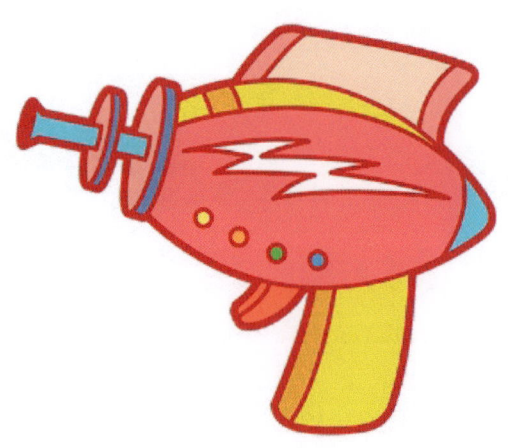

We played with a water gun.

sheep   mouton

Schaf

oveja   овца

The sheep have fluffy wool.

leg   jambe

Bein

pierna   ножка

My leg is feeling better.

man   homme

Mann

hombre   мужчина

This man is my dad.

door	porte

Tür

puerta	дверь

He is knocking on the door.

---

apple	pomme

Apfel

manzana	яблоко

Apples are a popular fruit.

---

sister	sœur

Schwester

hermana	сестра

She is my sister.

school	école
colegio	школа

Schule

They are going to school.

hand	main
mano	рука

Hand

You should wash your hands.

paper	papier
papel	бумага

Papier

I like to color on paper.

children   les enfants

Kinder

niños   дети

The children are playing.

chart   graphique

Diagramm

gráfico   диаграмма

What does your medical chart say?

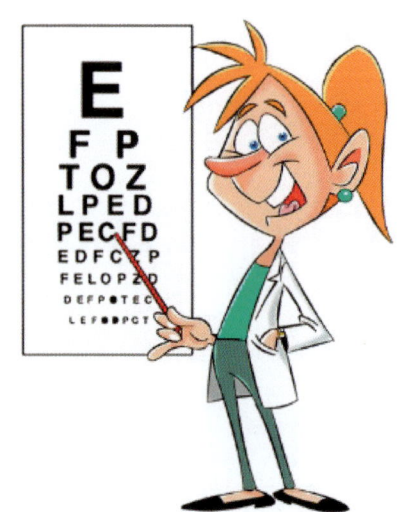

letter   alphabet

Alphabet

alfabeto   алфавит

Learn English letters is fun.

boat bateau

Boot

barco лодка

The boat is sailing.

---

birthday anniversaire

Geburtstag

cumpleaños рождения

Today is my birthday.

---

stick bâton

Stock

palo прут

He is playing sticks.

squirrel	écureuil

Eichhörnchen

ardilla	белка

The squirrel is on the tree.

---

rope	corde

Seil

cuerda	верёвка

Do you have any rope?

---

column	colonne

Säule

columna	колонка

Did you read the newspaper column?

face visage

Gesicht

cara лицо

They were at the face painting booth.

---

city ville

Stadt

ciudad город

He worked in the city.

---

farmer fermier

Farmer

agricultor фермер

The farmer had a farm.

floor		sol
Fußboden		
suelo		этаж

The girl sits on the floor.

watch		l'horloge
Uhr		
reloj		Часы

My watch is ticking.

wood		bois
Holz		
madera		дерево

He plays with wooden blocks

rabbit   lapin

Hase

conejo   кролик

The rabbit wants to play.

corn   blé

Mais

maíz   кукуруза

I grow corn in the garden.

time   temps

Zeit

hora   время

He is telling the time.

night	nuit

Nacht

noche	ночь

We sleep at night.

---

ring	bague

Ring

anillo	кольцо

The bird is holding a ring.

---

children	les enfants

Kinder

niños	дети

Four children sang.

pig porc

Schwein

cerdo свинья

She is lying on the pig.

---

baby bébé

Baby

bebé детка

The baby is crawling.

---

house maison

Haus

casa жилой дом

We live in the same house.

bed		lit
Bett		
cama		постель

We all share three beds.

flower		fleur
Blume		
flor		цветок

She is holding a flower.

egg		oeuf
Ei		
huevo		яйцо

The bunny has many eggs.

fire	feu
Feuer	
fuego	Пожар

Fire is hot.

---

day	journée
Tag	
día	день

This day is the 30th.

---

bird	oiseau
Vogel	
pájaro	птица

The bird is dancing happily.

men	hommes
Männer	
hombres	люди

The men are arguing.

seat	siège
Sitz	
asiento	сиденье

The girls took a seat in the sand.

garden	jardin
Garten	
jardín	сад

They are going to the garden.

Printed in Poland
by Amazon Fulfillment
Poland Sp. z o.o., Wrocław